The Woman's Game...

Power Volleyball

ANDY BANACHOWSKI
COACH WOMEN'S POWER VOLLEYBALL
U.C.L.A. BRUINS

A SPORTS PUBLICATION BY THE ATHLETIC INSTITUTE

THE ATHLETIC INSTITUTE
200 Castlewood Drive
North Palm Beach, FL 33408
U.S.A.

All photo credits:
Norm Schindler, ASUCLA Studio

Demonstrators:
UCLA Bruins

Published by The Athletic Institute
200 Castlewood Drive
North Palm Beach, Florida 33408
Printed in the United States of America

Library of Congress Catalog Card Number 82-74326
ISBN 87670-068-7

A WORD FROM THE PUBLISHER

THIS SPORTS PUBLICATION, is but one item in a comprehensive list of sports instructional aids, such as video cassettes, 16mm films, 8mm silent loops and filmstrips which are made available by The Athletic Institute. This book is part of a master plan which seeks to make the benefits of athletics, physical education and recreation available to everyone.

The Athletic Institute is a not-for-profit organization devoted to the advancement of athletics, physical education and recreation. The Institute believes that participation in athletics and recreation has benefits of inestimable value to the individual and to the community.

The nature and scope of the many Institute programs are determined by a Professional Advisory Committee, whose members are noted for their outstanding knowledge, experience and ability in the fields of athletics, physical education and recreation.

The Institute believes that through this book the reader will become a better performer, skilled in the fundamentals of this fine event. Knowledge and the practice necessary to mold knowledge into playing ability are the keys to real enjoyment in playing any game or sport.

Howard J. Bruns
President and Chief Executive Officer
The Athletic Institute

Dustin Cole
Executive Director
The Athletic Institute

CONTENTS

INTRODUCTION

The first contact is normally a pass to the setter.

Introduction

A Short History

Volleyball originated in the United States around the turn of the century and became a popular game in the YMCAs. During the war, soldiers carried the game to Europe with them where it was widely accepted. When volleyball was introduced as an Olympic sport in 1964 by the Japanese, the Americans were taught a lesson in the game they devised. America's participation in the Olympics has been sporadic, but our hopes for a medal are high in the 1984 Games. The sport has become a favorite in women's collegiate and high school athletic programs. Volleyball has experienced tremendous growth at these levels, and will continue to do so because of the excitement and action of the game.

How the Game is Played

Play is begun by a server hitting the ball over the net. The receiving team (each team has 6 players) then has three contacts (4 if the first contact was with your blockers) to return the ball over the net. Although it is not necessary to use all three contacts, it is usually wise to do so in order to obtain control of the ball and set up your attack. These three contacts will usually include a (1) pass to the net area, a (2) set to an attacker, and a (3) spike across the net. The object is to hit the ball to the floor in the opponent's court area.

Points may only be scored by the serving team, and the receiving team may only earn a side-out, which is the right to serve. The game is played to 15 points, with the winner needing a two-point advantage.

The pass is followed by a set and a hit.

Equipment and Rules

The equipment needed to play volleyball is relatively simple; the rules are not always so. The basic equipment required is a volleyball, a net strung tautly at the correct height between two poles, and some boundary markers. Players' equipment includes a jersey, shorts, a pair of kneepads, and a good pair of shoes. All equipment should be designed and maintained with the safety of the players in mind.

The court itself is a 9 by 18-meter rectangle, with the net dividing the court into two 9 x 9-meter squares. A 3-meter line is drawn on each side to restrict back court attackers.

The minimum ceiling height is 26 feet. A six-foot minimum clearance is recommended. Lines are within the court area and a ball landing on the line is good. For younger players it is recommended that the net height be placed just above the reach of the average player. The court looks like this:

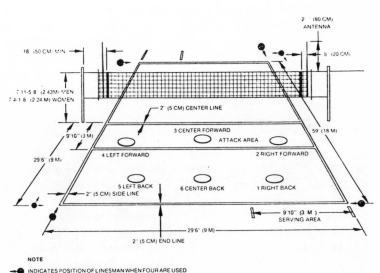

NOTE

●— INDICATES POSITION OF LINESMAN WHEN FOUR ARE USED
●— INDICATES POSITION OF LINESMAN WHEN TWO ARE USED

The rules in the United States are governed by the United States Volleyball Association (USVBA) which has adopted the international rules governed by the International Volleyball Federation (FIVB). That's one reason for the metric measurements of the court. NAGWS has written a set of rules for the college level, while high school rules are written by the National High School Federation. There has been an effort to have a common set of rules, but occasionally one of these groups forgets their good intentions and confusion reigns. The current major difference in the rules is the substitution rule where, in collegiate and high school girls play, you are allowed 12 substitutions total (3 entries per player). USVBA rules allow only 6 subs total (1 entry per player), but these differences are commonly accepted as a benefit to the collegiate and high school sports programs.

Basically the rules state that the ball cannot come to rest during any of the three contacts. The ball must be "cleanly" handled or hit, and may not be held or double hit.

Only players in the front court may attack or block the ball. Blockers may reach over the net but may not contact the ball on the other side of the net until the attack is made. Spikers may only cross the net on their follow-through. It is illegal to touch the net. Backcourt players may only attack the ball from the line which is three meters from the net (backline players' spiking line).

A team is allowed two 30-second time-outs per game. Players must be in proper rotational order during the serve, but may change positions immediately after the serve.

Contact your appropriate governing body to obtain a copy of the current rules.

The intent of this book is not to discuss rules, but the techniques and tactics of playing power volleyball. The first section covers the basic skills of volleyball, serving, passing and some movement. These skills will enable you to play the game and, at any level of play, are the determining factor between evenly matched teams.

The Advanced Skills section will cover setting, spiking, blocking, and some more movement skills. This section deals with the more exciting skills of volleyball.

The Team Skills section will deal with offenses and defenses and how to work together with your teammates on the court.

The final sections will deal with practicing, some drills, and some advice that will help you to be a better athlete and volleyball player.

Read on and enjoy!

Basic Skills

The Serve

The serve is the first of the basic skills that I will deal with in this book, not only because it is used to initiate the action of the game, but also because of its potential for determining the outcome. The importance of the serve should not be overlooked, since without this skill you will be unable to score points. A player who has developed a strong serve becomes a very valuable asset to the team, and will play an important role in its success. Studies have shown that over a wide spectrum of competition, the team with the most effective serve wins approximately three out of four games.

A strong serve should be consistent, accurate, and difficult to pass. It should be capable of scoring points (aces), or making it hard for the opponents to run their offense. These characteristics are developed through careful execution and lots of practice.

In executing the skill of the serve, I stress a minimum of movement since there is less chance for error in the fewer moves that you will make. For the basic FLOATER SERVE, take a comfortable stride-stance position behind the end line in the designated serving area. Your feet should be shoulder-width apart and pointing directly at your intended target, with the foot opposite your serving arm leading your stance. The stride-stance position allows you to maintain balance and still generate power through your arm-swing.

To begin the serving action, hold the ball with both hands directly in front of you above waist level. I recommend placing your serving hand on top of the ball and positioning your non-serving arm directly under the ball, allowing it to rest in your hand. You will want to make the toss of the ball in front of your serving arm. The toss is very important in developing consistency and accuracy in your serve.

Begin by lifting the arms in a deliberate motion, bringing the ball over to the serving arm side of your body. As the upward motion continues, your serving hand will come off the ball and begin to draw back in preparation for the armswing. The non-serving arm continues to lift the ball upwards, releasing it with a gentle flick of the wrist so the ball will continue its upward flight to a position above and in front of your shoulder. The toss should not be too high or it will cause timing problems with your armswing.

As you're making an accurate toss, the serving arm is drawn back behind the head with the hand in an upward position. During this action your weight has shifted to the back foot of your stride stance and the ball is released in the toss.

A rotation of the shoulder should initiate the forward movement of your armswing. This allows you to lead your swing with your elbow which will create a stronger swing as you straighten your arm. From this position your weight begins to shift forward as you swing. Many players prefer to take a step forward with the lead foot to accomplish this weight shift, but no more than one step should be taken. This action also helps to align the shoulder and arm for proper contact with the ball. Your arm should extend upward (not complete extension) and forward to make contact with your hand on the ball. The armswing must be a fast forward action and not a deliberate or guiding movement.

You should make contact at the mid-point of the ball (remember you're trying to serve a floater), imagining that you are driving your hand straight through the ball. Contact is made with the flat of the hand which is held in an upright position, although much of the force will be imparted with the heel of the hand. Because we are trying to make the ball "float" across the net, it is necessary to maintain the

wrist in a rigid position throughout the contact and follow-through.

The follow-through is minimal, but should follow the path of the ball, while the hand is maintained in an upright position and the wrist is rigid. The transfer of weight forward is completed with the follow-through, and then allows you to quickly move to your designated defensive position on the court.

Technique Review
> **Comfortable stride stance with feet pointing at target area.**
> **Accurate toss in front of serving arm.**
> **Fast arm action starting from behind head.**
> **Rigid wrist.**
> **Minimal follow-through**

There are other types of serves which can be used, but the basic principles described already should still apply.

An UNDERHAND SERVE can be used for beginning players or when a change of pace in your serving is needed. The toss (more of a drop) is made at wrist level as the swinging arm moves through an underhand arc. Primary contact is with the heel of the hand, and sometimes the fingers may be curled into a fist to lend more force. The follow-through is more pronounced to get the necessary strength and height on the ball to clear the net.

An even more effective change of pace serve is a TOP-SPIN SERVE. This ball is designed to drop quickly in front of the passer because of the excessive amount of spin. This is a very effective serve, but should become easy to pass once it is recognized because of its predictable flight path.

To make this type of serve, the ball should be contacted at a point above and slightly behind the shoulder. Contact is made on the bottom half of the ball and the wrist is snapped vigorously upward and forward at contact to impart the necessary spin. A more pronounced follow-through adds more speed and spin to the ball.

Tactics

Remembering the importance of the serve (you can't score points without serving the ball), it seems obvious that you should concentrate extremely hard to perform the skills correctly and serve the ball in the court. Yet because the player is spotlighted during this part of the game, often the pressure of the moment affects the outcome of the much-rehearsed skills. It is necessary to maintain your composure whenever serving.

Some simple guidelines can easily improve your serving effectiveness. It is most important to make sure that the serve will be good (in). The best possible serve is a combination of strength and accuracy.

To make your serve more difficult to pass, serve to an open spot on the court, or serve near the net, or in the deep corners where it is more difficult to pass the ball.

When serving, look for a weak passer, a nervous player, or someone who has just made an error. Also serve someone who has just been substituted into the game, or a player who is upset or one who is talking to the referee, a coach, or is distracted by the crowd.

It is often effective to change your serving tactics, such as serving long, short, and then long again; or to change from your normal serve and use a different serve, such as the overhand top-spin serve. If you normally serve from the end line, you can back up to change your serve. Serving into the path of the setter or serving the opponent's best spiker can often disrupt your opponent's offensive strategy.

These tactics should be employed only after you have mastered control of your serve, and practice them enough to give you confidence to use them effectively.

You must also be able to recognize at what points during the game it is wise to use varying tactics. It is always important to serve the ball in, but a no-risk in serve is called for after the opponents call a time-out or make a substitution, or after a teammate's serving error, or when the game is close. You may run the risk of a more difficult serve when your team is way ahead or way behind, or near the end of the game (but only one).

Every player should develop serves to each area of the court (line, crosscourt, short, and deep) that are both accurate and difficult to pass. As you practice these skills, emphasis should be placed on control and consistency just as if you were serving in a game.

Forearm Passing

Forearm passing is the second of the two basic skills that, when mastered, will allow you to successfully play volleyball. It probably is the most important one since failure to execute this skill in service receive will result in loss of point. This skill is used most often to receive serve and to dig the opponent's spikes, but can also be used to set the ball to your teammates and to "bump" the ball over the net when that is your only option left. With slight modifications of the basic technique, this skill can be used to pass, set, and dig. While different coaches will teach different fundamentals for its performance, there are some basic principles that should be followed.

Serve Receive

The basic action of the forearm pass is to bring your arms together and play the ball off the forearm surface of your arms. It is important to keep the ball in front of you as you move to the ball and establish yourself in a position whereby you will be able to intercept the flight of the ball and direct it to your target. In all cases it is advisable to arrive at that position before the ball and assume your passing position. In simplest terms, move quickly and get ready to pass.

When you get into position to pass the ball, you should assume a passing stance that will allow you flexibility to make any last-second corrections to the flight of the ball. I recommend the use of a stride

A comfortable stride stance allows movement to the ball when passing a free ball, although a wider stance is recommended for serve reception and digging.

stance with an exaggerated width. The feet should be wider than shoulder width yet still maintaining a lead foot to give direction and allow for necessary weight shifts and movement. In serve receiving and digging, the stance will be wider than that used in a free ball passing situation or a setting situation. The wider stance should allow for stability yet not decrease the mobility that is necessary.

Most players will have a tendency to favor a particular foot in the lead position, but I am not convinced that this is an absolute necessity when passing the ball. I do believe this is more important (right foot forward on right side of court, left foot forward on left side of court) when playing defense (digging) since your reaction time is limited by the speed of the spiked ball, and your ability to effect desired body control is reduced.

As you take this position you may bring your hands together in any of a variety of ways, whichever is most comfortable for the player. One method is to interlock the fingers and place the thumbs side by side. Another method is to make a fist with one hand and wrap the other hand around it, again aligning the thumbs side by side. A third method, although less commonly used, is to merely lay one hand in a palms up position inside the other, again aligning the thumbs side by side.

In all of these methods, the proper alignment of the thumbs is a key to making a good passing surface with the forearms. The thumbs should also be pointed in a downward direction towards the floor to ensure that the elbows will be locked (the arms extended away from

the body), and that a flat even surface will be maintained throughout the passing action.

You should strive to make contact with the ball at a point directly in line with the middle of your body in front of you. The ball should be played from a position between, but in front of, your knees.

Contact with the ball is made on the forearms at a point above the wrists. Contact too close to the wrists is more difficult to control because of the unevenness of the surface and contact too high on the forearms often results in a double hit or lifting violation being whistled.

The basic idea of the forearm pass is to present to the ball a large, relatively flat platform from which it may rebound. The ball is usually played with the wide, somewhat flat area of the outwardly rotated forearms about halfway between the wrists and the elbows. This platform must be at the appropriate angle upon contact with the ball so that the ball may rebound to the target at the desired height.

Contact is initiated by generating a forward movement to the ball through the legs via a weight shift (to the forward foot which is pointed at the target). This gentle momentum is carried through to the body to the arms where a slight swinging action of the arms gives the necessary impetus and direction to the ball. The arm action should stop at shoulder level and normally begins at waist level. The arms remain together throughout the passing motion and follow-through.

Other methods may emphasize more armswing and less body movement to achieve the desired angles and positioning for passing, but a combination of arm and leg movement allows for more flexibili-

ty, stability, and range throughout the passing motion.

The pass is completed with a follow-through of the body in a direct line to the target. The legs straighten from the crouch or semi-crouch (bent position) as the arms extend forward.

Technique Review

Move to the ball, keeping it directly in front of you.

Assume passing position with legs bent, arms together in front of you away from the body.

Align yourself to the target area.

Lock hands together, thumbs to the floor.

Even contact on forearms.

Pass with lifting action of arms and legs.

Complete follow-through to target area.

Tactics

The ball should be passed to the setter in a looping manner so that it will drop into her hands in a position just in front of the setter to allow her to move to the ball. The ball should not be passed too low, nor should it be passed too high, too close to, or over the net. A target area, usually to the right of center, should be established, and all passes directed to this area.

If you're unable to position yourself directly behind the ball (you're not being lazy, are you?) or keep the ball in front of you, with a slight modification of technique you can still accurately pass the ball.

For the ball that keeps coming at you at chest level, you must quickly step aside or turn sideways, rotate the shoulders and lift the arms

to contact the ball. Having pulled your chest out of the way, drop your front shoulder to properly angle your arms to direct the flight of the ball to the target.

For that ball that is to your side, step to the ball while you bring your arms up, extending them to contact the ball. The important thing to remember again is to lower the front shoulder to stop the flight of the ball and redirect it to your target area.

Dig-Defense

The forearm passing technique is similarly used in the dig. The dig is a defensive technique to play the attack shot of the opponent once it has passed by the block. The forearm pass technique must be slightly modified to successfully accomplish a dig.

Because of the speed and angle of the spike, the defensive ready position for the dig must be necessarily lower and allow for quickness. Again a wide stride stance is recommended but positioned so that the outside foot (nearest to sideline) is forward. Often the spike travels with such velocity that it does not allow any time for adjustments of body position. Thus with the body aligned facing into the court before the spike, the possibility of a successful dig to your teammates is assured.

The defensive position must be low with the knees bent. The weight must be forward (on the balls of your feet) to allow you to move. Your knees should be forward of your feet and slightly angled inwards, your elbows forward of your knees and your hands extended forward, but not yet clasped together in the forearm pass position. This will allow you quickly to react to the ball.

As the ball is spiked, you must react and move to dig the ball.

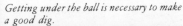
The arms must soften the dig.

Getting under the ball is necessary to make a good dig.

11

Control of the dig is essential and every effort should be made to play the ball with both arms. Before contact the arms are clasped together and already extended away from the body. Because the speed of the ball is so great, very little, if any, forward movement through the contact with the ball is necessary. Most often a cushioning or softening attempt must be made. At contact the cushioning is effected by allowing the ball to "push your arms back toward your body." Because of this softening, the "follow-through" is in the reverse direction and therefore the proper body position before the contact is extremely important. Weight forward is important in the ready position to allow for quick movement (you're ready for the dink, aren't you?), and to accomplish this reverse follow-through or softening effect on the ball. Unfortunately, the dig is most often not executed under these ideal conditions and less than ideal body positions are necessary to play the ball.

The forearm passing skill can also be used to set the ball to your teammate or to bump the ball over the net to your opponents. Although there are more preferred skills to use in setting and returning the ball, this technique should not be overlooked to make a saving play or to make an easy play out of a difficult one. This is especially true when the setter cannot quite get into proper position to set the ball; rather than risk mis-handling the ball, a forearm or "bump" set should be used.

Basic Movement

As mentioned, volleyball is a game of movement, and as the ball moves back and forth around the court and across the net, the players must be constantly moving to adjust their positions to play the ball.

Essential to any positioning on the court is forward and backward movement. Quick forward movement is accomplished simply by running to the desired position.

Backward movement is easily done by simply running backwards ("backpedaling"). Using a backward lean while backpedaling will quicken the movement.

Sideways movement is also essential to cover the court, and while it is possible (and recommended for long distances) to turn and run, quick side movements can be made by using the "slide step" or the "crossover step."

In the slide step, the fast movement is made by the lead foot. It moves in the desired direction (e.g., right foot to the right) without turning. The other foot slides alongside the lead foot. If you have reached your desired position then your final stepping action is made by the lead foot into a comfortable stance to prepare for your next action. A continuation of the "lead step-slide" action can be used to move greater distances. The slide step is most commonly used by defensive players moving into position to dig or pass the ball. It is also used by blockers to move along the net and position themselves for a block.

To further quicken this movement, a similar step-hop action can be used. The first movement is with the lead foot, and from this wide stance position a sideways hop is executed to place you in the desired position and stance for your next action.

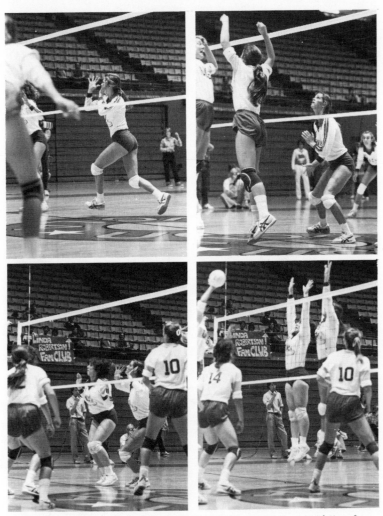

The crossover step is most often used by middle blockers to "get inside" to form a double block.

The crossover step can be used to cover greater distances more quickly. It is most frequently used by middle blockers as they hurriedly move into position to block, and sometimes by backcourt defenders when they have a greater distance to move.

The crossover step is initiated by the lead foot stepping and turning, (the body will turn partially also, but the shoulders should not open excessively), and taking a lengthy stride. The second step is the cross-over as the trail foot passes the position of the first step. This is a vigorous step and should cover a great distance. As this step is being made, the body should begin pivoting (while in the air) back to its original position as the foot lands. Finally a third step is made by the lead foot as it is planted (to stop the sideways movement) to bring the body back around to complete the movement and put the player in position for the next action whether it be a jumping action to block or preparing to dig.

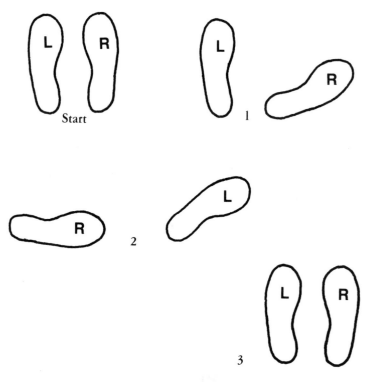

Advanced Skills

Overhead Pass

The overhand pass is an extremely important skill to master because of its use. It is used primarily to "set" the ball for your teammate to spike, and can be used to pass a "free ball" (an easy pass) or return the ball over the net. Its first use, the set, is its most important function since good setting greatly enchances your team's attacking ability.

When attempting the overhand pass, positioning yourself is very important. You must be able to anticipate the point at which you will intercept the flight of the ball and beat the ball to that spot. You want to place yourself at a point where the ball will be above and slightly in front of your forehead.

When you arrive at this spot you want to assume a stride stance position (right foot forward) with the feet about shoulder width apart. This will provide you with mobility and stability. It is often helpful to make a little jump-step into this position, which helps put the weight on the toes and creates a slight flexion of the knees. Otherwise the rest of the body is fairly erect.

As the ball approaches, the hands should come up together to meet the ball at the contact point (above the head). The hands should be shaped to fit the contour of the ball, and the elbows should be raised and positioned slightly above and outside of the shoulders. This should

be a comfortable position with the hands four to six inches above the forehead.

Look for the ball through the "window" that is formed by your thumbs and forefingers as you wait in this ready position.

Contact is made with the pads of your fingers and thumbs, and wrap around the ball as it descends into your hands. Although most of the contact is made with the first two fingers of each hand, all the fingers should be extended to absorb the contact of the ball. The wrists should be cocked and ready to flex back in order to achieve the proper absorption of the ball. Additional flexion is provided at the elbows. Don't hit or bat the ball, but try to soften the contact.

To release the ball, the wrists are snapped upward and forward as the elbows straighten out to provide the necessary distance and direc-

tion to the ball. Additional force for a lengthy set is provided by the legs with the knees straightening and adding to the follow-through.

The follow-through is completed with a simultaneous straightening of the entire body in the direction of the ball. The fingers should be followed in the flight of the ball with the wrists maintaining a position in line with the arms. A strong follow-through will see the setter rise to her toes and often come completely off the ground.

Technique Review

Position self in stride stance before arrival of ball.

Raise hands above head to meet ball.

Sight ball through window with hands shaped to fit ball.

Soften contact by absorbing ball, don't hit it.

Release ball with flexion of wrists.

Hands straight forward after contact.

Complete action with smooth follow-through of body and arms in one movement.

To perform the back set (an overhand pass to a spot behind you), the same basic techniques can be used. It is important to position yourself the same, so as not to give away the direction of your set until the last possible moment.

The back set is begun by sliding the hips forward and arching the back on contact with the ball. Then the ball is released in a direction behind the head, while the body and arms complete the follow-through in that direction.

An overhand pass may be used to pass a "free ball." Using the overhand pass can increase the accuracy of your pass and speed up your team's offensive action. The same techniques are used, but the back may be slightly angled forward since you are passing the ball in a lower trajectory. This allows you to still line the ball up on the forehead and complete the pass as before.

This same technique can also be used to return the ball to your opponents if it is your third contact and you're unable to spike the ball.

Setters must be able to jump set to save close passes, speed up the offense, and/or fool opposing blockers.

Tactics

When setting the ball, you must always try to make the best possible set for your attacker to spike. You should be able to set to any position along the net, and set a variety of sets. This will determine your team's style of play.

Sets are generally named according to a coach's preference with numbers or letters, and include high sets, outside "shoot" sets, and inside "quick" sets.

The one-set is a quick set that depends on excellent timing between the setter and the hitter. The hitter should jump before, or as, the setter is setting the ball, depending on the speed of the style you adopt. The setter must put the ball directly in front of the attacker so she may quickly hit the ball. This play is designed to out-quick rather than overpower the defense, and is often used as a fake to set up your other hitters. It is normally set in front but some very advanced offenses will also run it behind the setter.

The two-set is a higher set, traveling 2-3 feet above the net. It may

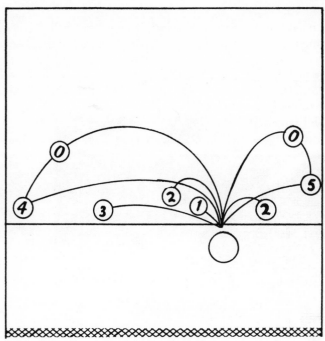

be set forward or back (the hitter does not jump until after the set is made).

A three-set is a low inside shoot set, usually set to a spot 10 feet from the left sideline. The trajectory of this set (flat or with a loop) may vary depending on your style of play.

A four-set is an outside shoot set, usually with a loop, that travels to the end of the court. This same set backwards is often called a five-set.

A high outside set is called a regular or 0-set. This set is most frequently used and should be mastered from any part of the court. It travels in a high arc (8-10' above the net) that should allow the ball to drop into the hitter's range.

Sets should not be too close to the net (1-2' off), and better setters will be able to make slight adjustments to suit each hitter. Generally taller players require higher sets.

Sets coming from the backcourt area should be slightly more inside and off the net to allow the hitter a better opportunity to attack successfully.

An accomplished setter knows which hitter should be getting the ball in each situation, and should be prepared to capitalize on a weakness in the opponents' front line. Skilled setters will also hide their sets and/or try to fool the blockers so that they can isolate their hitters against a single or no blocker.

Spike

Spiking is generally the most exciting part of volleyball and distinguishes power volleyball from recreational volleyball. The thrill of spiking is overwhelming, and this skill is one that players continually want to practice.

The successful spike is composed of different parts which include: the approach, the jump, the armswing, contact with the ball, the follow-through and landing. These are dependent on good basic foundations in running, jumping and throwing. Timing is also critical. It is necessary for most beginning volleyball players to practice these basic movement patterns separately before becoming effective spikers.

Positioning is critical for a good spike and you want to begin your approach from a position just off the net. Most players will start from 10-15 feet off the net so they can generate speed throughout their approach.

The action must begin with a good pass made to the setter. Mentally gauge the flight of the set to be in proper position at the proper time to contact the ball at the maximum height of the jump.

From the ready position make any minor corrections in approach necessary because of an inaccurate set. The spiker normally waits until the ball leaves the setter's hands, then explodes for the approach and jump.

The most commonly used approach is the step-close approach where the spiker will take 4 steps to approach the ball. I recommend that players take a 4 step approach, and make their first step with the same foot as their hitting arm. That is, a right-handed spiker will take her first step with the right foot, and the last (closing) step will be with the foot opposite the spiking arm. The approach will be right-left, right-left.

The last step is a closing step and should bring you into a position to begin your jump. This step should bring your feet nearly paralled (most players have a tendency to overstep the closing step and turn the foot sideways) with both feet pointing into the opponent's court. The last two steps must be quick to build up speed.

The hop approach is similar at the beginning but varies at the end. After taking 2 or 3 steps, the player will push off the last step to a two-foot simultaneous landing with a short hopping action. This will put the player in a position to begin her jump. The hopping action is a pre-jump and should not be a high hop; rather it should be low and quick, and put you in position to jump and attack.

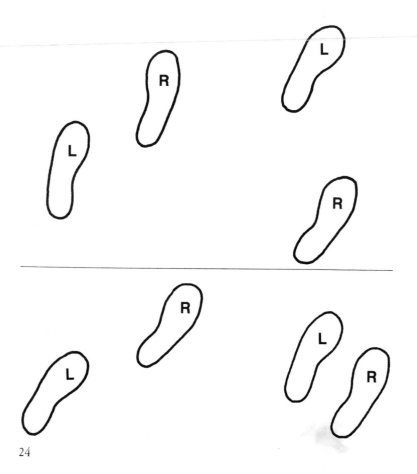

JUMP — In order to get a maximum jump, it is important to learn proper techniques and use them in your spike. As you make the last steps or the hop in your approach, you want to convert some of your forward momentum into upward momentum. To do this you should emphasize a heel-first landing of your last steps (or hop) while maintaining a slight backward body lean. Keeping your hips behind your heels will help maintain this body position. The arms must also be drawn behind you in preparation for an upward swing through the jumping action. The arms are drawn back on your right step and come forward on your left closing step. To jump you should allow your body to swing forward as you rock from your heels to your toes to make an explosive

A straight approach is recommended from the off-hand side of the court.

jump. The knees must be bent so that the player is in a crouching position just before the jump. To maximize your jump, you should remember to make your jumping actions quick and drive off the floor with as much force as you can generate from your legs through your ankles, feet and toes.

As you jump in the air you're ready to begin your armswing action as your arms reach your eye level. Your hitting arm should be drawn back behind your head as your non-hitting arm continues upward to find the ball. This helps to maintain balance and create power throughout the swing in addition to helping you jump. To begin the forward swing, you should rotate your shoulder so that your elbow will lead your swing. Your non-hitting arm begins to drop as you begin your swing. With your elbow leading, your arm extends upward and forward to contact the ball at the desired attack point, which most often is above and in front of your attacking shoulder. Your arm should unleash, as a whip uncoiling, to make contact. Contact is made with the heel of the hand as the entire hand wraps over the ball to impart the necessary topspin to drive the ball down into the court. This is done by cocking the wrist prior to contact and vigorously snapping the wrist on contact with the ball. To gain additional power in your spikes the body should also snap forward from your waist using a vigorous action of the stomach muscles.

The closer the ball is to the net and the higher the contact, the more the point of contact should be on the top side of the ball. The farther the ball is from the net and the lower the point of contact, the

more the contact should be made from behind and below the ball. Thus the high or close contact is hit from in front of your body whereas the low or away contact is hit directly over your body.

Although many coaches prefer a natural follow-through with the arm, at the learning stages I recommend a straight ahead follow-through, with the arm and hand passing by the side of the body. This will help the beginning player to learn control of the spike. There will obviously be times when this must be altered, such as with a close set, and the follow-through must be stopped or brought across the body to prevent a "net."

Your landing completes your spike and should be balanced and cushioned. Your knees should flex as much as in the take-off in order to absorb the shock to the body. You should land on both feet and be ready for the next action, whether it is to cover your own blocked spike or to prepare to block your opponents'.

Technique Review
> Move off the net.
> Fast approach.
> Two-foot jump with heel to toe rock.
> Arms lift.
> Hitting arm back.
> Rotate shoulder.
> Elbow leads arm swing.
> Vigorous contact on ball.
> Wrist snap to give topspin.
> Follow-through and soft landing.

Tactics

Players must learn and know the basic principles. You should also realize that each individual has different jumping and hitting techniques, but they should be developed within these general basic principles. Differences in techniques often create difficulties for your opponents, so do not be afraid to develop your own style and correct technique.

In order to attack effectively, you must always be in a good position to use your attacking skills. It is important to learn to hit the ball hard, but it is more important to learn to use correct technique. Players must learn to attack around the block and to weak defensive areas of the court. An attacker must choose from the many possibilities and decide on the best one to use at the moment of attack.

Players should learn to hit the ball high over the net by utilizing a maximum jump and extending the arm to spike. The higher you jump to attack the ball, the greater exist the angles and possibilitites of attack.

Players who develop quick armswings should try and beat the block, while players with slower armswings should use more attack variations.

You should always try to approach and jump in the same way, and only change your angles of attack by changing your arm swing, upper body, wrist, or attack point on the ball.

Although the approach should be the same, there are some guidelines I recommend. When attacking from the on-hand side (the ball comes to the attacking arm before crossing the body), I suggest the use of an angled approach. This means that the player should slide-step to a position outside the court and approach to the attack point on a slight angle. This should prevent a wide set from crossing her body and giving the spiker no armswing or no court to hit.

From the off-hand side (ball must cross body before spiker approaches) I recommend the use of a straight approach. This puts the spiker in a better position to attack the entire court and to get to an inside set before it drops too low.

You should be able to attack all parts of the court and the block to become a good spiker. In order to move the ball around the court, either crosscourt or line, a simple method is to move the contact point of the ball. The normal contact point is above and in front of the shoulder. Attacking from the power side (on-hand) you can hit a crosscourt spike by contacting the ball slightly outside the shoulder. To hit the line (always aim 1-2' inside the line), let the ball come inside your shoulder or in front of your face before you contact it. To hit a sharp (inside) crosscourt angle you can let the ball drop low (not below the net) and outside the shoulder before you make contact.

You can also change your angle of attack by turning your upper body in the air. This will be more recognizable to the defenders, but nevertheless can be very effective. Turning the wrist on contact with the ball is another effective method of changing your angles of attack.

Mis-hitting the ball is often an accidental means of changing the attack, but can just as easily be done purposely. Rather than contacting the ball in the middle, attack the ball on the left half to drive it to the right.

Any of these techniques can be successfully used to vary your attack, but do not use too many at the same time and expect to be able to control the ball and hit it in the court.

When attacking against a block, do not let yourself be intimidated by its presence. You must be aware of it and choose your shots wisely. It is essential to be able to see the block, and this is one reason you want to keep the ball in front of you while attacking. You should look for weakness in the block to attack, such as a short blocker, a player who blocks off the net, or a hole in the block. A common place to attack a double block is the seam between the blockers. Often the seam is not properly closed and a hard-driven spike will find its way through to the floor.

Another effective method of attacking the block is to hit a high flat shot off the top of the blocker's hands. This can be hit at the seam or off a single blocker. To hit this shot you must keep your elbow lower through the swing so you do not come over the top of the ball.

A good spiker will practice all shots and will always try to hit every ball in practice. This will be a good training for turning mis-plays into points or side-outs in a game. Just because the ball is not set right at the net does not mean you cannot attack it. As long as you get yourself in good position, you should attempt to spike.

If the ball is set deep of the net, you can still attack effectively by moving the contact point directly above your shoulder and hitting the ball on the bottom half while imparting a lot of topspin. This will drive the ball over the net and down into the court.

A good spiker will also try to spike the ball that is being set to the net from the backcourt area. Rather than turning your back to the net and waiting to bump the ball over the net, you must quickly get off the net and position yourself outside the court so that you can take an angled approach. This will allow you to approach and attack while still being able to see the ball and the opposing blockers. If you don't use an angled approach, you will end up trying to hit a ball coming over your shoulder, which is very difficult to do.

Changing the speed of your attack can be another effective way of adding variety to your attack. This can be done with a combination of off-speed spikes and open-hand dink shots.

The off-speed spike is similar to a deep spike in that you want the contact point above your shoulder and to attack the ball on the lower side. Here you should slow down the armswing while quickly snapping the wrist on contact to impart topspin and direction to the ball.

The open-hand dink should also look like your normal spike until the moment of contact, since its effectiveness relies on surprise and accurate placement to an open spot on the court. Your armswing should stop at the top of your swing to make contact with your fingers on the ball. In an action similar to that used in overhand passing, with one hand you will absorb and release the ball with a flexion of the wrist. You should make the ball travel only high enough to get over the blockers, so that it will quickly drop to the floor.

Hitting play sets requires timing and coordination between the setter and spiker. Both players must have confidence in the other that they will perform their skills properly. Without these ingredients, a good play cannot be completed.

To hit "shoot" sets, attackers must adjust the timing of their approach to the quickness of the set, and be prepared to swing quickly at the ball before it passes them.

To hit quick middle sets, timing is essential, and requires much practice. The fastest middle hit has an attacker in the air as the ball is set and ready to swing. The emphasis is on quickness with this hit, and the elbow to hand action of the armswing must be emphasized. Often a "straighter" armswing will give the necessary height and quickness to make this hit effective.

The Block

The block is playing an increasingly important role in today's game of power volleyball. This is easily seen in the excitement generated by a well-timed block, the increasing height of today's volleyball player, and the employment of the block against the serve.

The block is the first line of defense against an opponent's attack and can be used offensively to block balls for a point, or considered defensively, to cover an area of the court and deflect balls to a team-mate. Your blocking style may be dictated by your size, your opponent's attack position, or the philosophy of your coach.

Blockers can and should be an intimidating force at the net that will cause much concern for the opposing spiker.

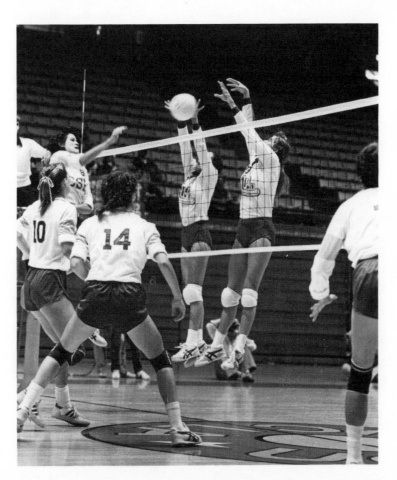

Single

To be an effective blocker you should take a good ready position at the net with your hands held forward no higher than your shoulders. (Any higher may cause you to be whistled for screening by the referee.) You may be at least one step off the net until you see that the opponent's pass is staying in their court. If the pass is coming over, you will be ready to step and spike the overpass. Smaller blockers may want to use this step to help increase their jump on the block, but this will sometimes cause timing and positioning problems when forming a double block.

You will want to watch your hitter to see if she is going to give away her attack plans early. You must watch the ball being set so that you will know where to position yourself to block. It is very important to maintain a wide field of vision so that you can watch the ball being set and the movement of your opposing hitters. Vision becomes more important in the air as you watch the hitter attack. You must train yourself not to blink during contact and learn to follow the flight of the ball after the block.

You should time your jump so that you will be in a position to intercept the ball as it is about to cross the net. You initiate your jumping action with a deep crouch by bending at the knees (not the waist) and making an explosive jumping action with the legs. The hands and arms should maintain a forward position and slide upward as you jump. Because you are so close to the net you do not want to swing your arms forward and upward as in the spike jump technique since this will lead to excessive net violations. At all times during the blocking action the hands should be forward of the face.

Blockers must maintain good vision throughout the blocking sequence.

Blockers should reach across the net.

Once in the air, extend the arms and hands forward to meet the oncoming ball. Blockers who can reach over the net should maximize their penetration to take away as many angles as possible, and prevent the ball from sliding under the block. This can be done by shrugging the shoulders and moving the head forward, but do not drop the head so low that you lose visual contact with the attacker.

I do not recommend snapping the wrists forward on contact, but prefer a rigid wrist maintained in line with the arms. This will provide enough of a downward rebound to the blocked ball, and may save a finger injury to an over-anxious blocker. The hands should be spread wide open from little finger to thumb to cover as much area as possible.

Shorter blockers can still be effective by blocking "straight up," thus in effect raising the height of the net. The use of a "soft-block" whereby the wrists are angled backwards allows the small blocker to effectively direct the ball to a teammate after it has crossed the net.

After you have completed your blocking action you must pull your arms and body away from the net to prevent a net violation. Remember to cushion your landing by bending your knees, and always try to keep your eyes on the ball. After you land (if the ball is still in play), quickly prepare yourself for the next action of the game, which usually will require a quick movement off the net to find the ball and prepare for an attack.

Double

A double block is formed when two players combine to form a block. Usually the middle blocker will move to join one of the two outside blockers. The middle blocker will often have to move quickly and will use the crossover step.

The crossover step is done the following way:

1. Make a short step with your lead foot.
2. Then make a large crossover step with the other foot, almost as if turning to run.
3. Stop your sideward momentum by planting your (original) trailing foot.
4. The lead foot rotates you into position. Plant your foot so that you are able to jump straight up while coordinating your jump with the stationary blocker's.

The outside blockers should slide-step into position.

The players must work together to form a wall of four hands above the net, and must time the jump together. If the block is poorly formed, defense of the court is nearly impossible. Most often the center blocker will have responsibility for closing the block (moving the hand to the seam of the block). The outside blocker has responsibility for turning the hitter in. This is done by angling the outside hand into the court and extending it slightly higher and farther over the net to prevent the spiker from hitting off the block. The "closing the block" responsibility can be given to the outside hitter if the attack position of the hitter or the team strategy of blocking more angle dictates such a tactic. However, this responsibility must be clearly understood at all times.

The outside blocker should angle the outside hand into the court, but not let the ball slip through the hands.

Responsibility for closing the block normally belongs to the middle blocker.

The outside blocker can be responsible for closing the block.

Technique Review

Ready position.

Watch the set.

Watch the spiker's approach.

Bend knees and jump after spiker.

Penetrate above net with hands and arms as you watch spiker's armswing movements.

Block the ball.

Pull back from net and cushion landing.

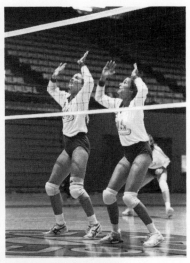

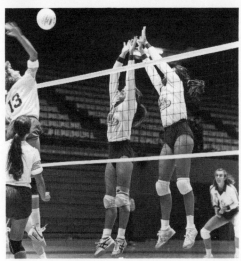

Tactics

Learn your opponent's favorite shots and block them. Make your hitter use a less desired shot.

Remember to delay your jump for a ball that is set off the net, or against a tall attacker, a good jumper, or one who has a slow armswing.

For a ball that slips under the block, wait until it has cleared the bottom of the net before you attempt to play it. Crouch low to the floor and wait until the ball is low to the floor before you try to play it.

For balls that are hit by the block, turn your head and watch the ball as you land and step off the net to get ready for the next play.

Advanced Movement

In this section I will deal with defensive techniques which allow a player to increase the range of movement on the court and consequently be in position to dig more balls. Keep in mind while discussing the techniques of the roll, the dive, and the sprawl, that you should always go after the ball with two hands and that you need to play the ball high enough in the air to allow your setter to get it.

A good defensive player will always be in good defensive position with weight forward and low to the floor. This will prevent a lot of bumps and bruises when going to the floor since the distance from your body to the floor will not be too great.

Often the ball will be beyond our normal range of movement and by using one of the following techniques we will be able to get a ball that would normally fall to the floor.

Roll

To perform a roll while digging a ball, you should move toward the ball with a slide-step action. Your last step should stretch you out

Extending your body parallel to floor to play the ball increases your range and softens the contact. Teammates' encouragement always helps also!

toward the ball as your body moves low to the floor. You should attempt to play the ball in front of you between your knees or if the ball is still beyond you at a 45 ° angle forward of your body. After contacting the ball as you go to the floor, you should pivot slightly on the extended foot as you sit back to the side of your buttocks. Allow your momentum to carry your weight across your back to the opposite shoulder. Continue this action by pulling your knees over this shoulder, tuck your chin on your chest, and push with your hands on the floor until your toes come in contact with the floor. At this point stand up and ready yourself for the next action. If you're rolling to the right, your right leg will stretch out, your right side will come in contact with the floor first, and then you will roll across your back to your left shoulder and over onto your feet.

You should always position yourself to be moving forward to perform this skill whether you are moving to your right or left or directly forward.

Roll Review
Stay low to the floor.
Extend your body with a long step.
Play the ball, preferably with both arms.
Pivot and contact floor.
Roll across back to opposite shoulder.
Pull knees over until feet contact floor.
Get up quickly for next action.

Dive
The dive will increase your range on the court even more dramatically since the skill is often performed from a run. However, the risk of injury is greater, unless the skill is performed correctly, and you have enough upper body strength to cushion your body's fall to

the floor. Also remember the original intent of the dive is to play the ball. Many players develop beautiful dives, but are never able to play the ball.

Every effort must be made to play the ball. Often the actual dive is not made until after contact with the ball has been completed, but is necessary because the player has extended her body so completely that it is the simplest way to recover. This is perfectly acceptable and results in the greatest number of successful diving digs.

Occasionally, the player will be completely airborne at the moment of contact with the ball, and this move requires more quickness and strength to get the ball up and recover to absorb your landing.

It is important to play the ball close to the floor when using a dive since that will be the height from which you fall to the floor. You want to be low to the floor as you extend your body forward. Your arms should extend out to make contact with the ball. Many times you will have to give some impetus to the ball either by swinging both arms up, or in desperation with a one-arm swing making contact with the back of the hand. If the ball is off to the side, a sidearm lifting swing, making contact on the forearm, will give a good lift to the ball.

You should push off with one foot from the floor in a forward direction, allowing your body to take a downward angle. It is after contact with the ball, if at all, that your foot breaks contact with the floor. Both feet should be above your head as your arms reach out to make contact with the floor. Your forward momentum will move your shoulders past your hand position on the floor as your arms lower your body to the floor. Your body should be arched and chin held up to avoid the floor as you land high on your stomach and slide through the landing. The slide absorbs the momentum from your dive. Your arms "push" you through the landing and then you must regain your feet to continue play. This skill must be practiced thoroughly so that the player's concern is the ball and not the floor.

Dive Review
> Stay low to the floor and move quickly.
> Extend to play the ball.
> Push off one foot to leave the floor.
> Angle the body downward so feet are above head.
> Hands on the floor to cushion and absorb landing.
> Push through as body makes contact with the floor.
> Get up quickly for next action.

Sprawl

The sprawl or "collapse dig" seems to be a refinement of the "sacrifice your body to get the ball" dig. It appears to be a combination of the dive and roll techniques where the body is always in contact with the floor as in the roll, and the body parallels the floor as in the dive. In any case it has developed into an excellent technique to dig the ball.

From a low defensive position the player quickly lunges forward (or to the side), stretching her body out parallel to the floor. Different techniques see (1) the body extending over the knee, (2) the knee pivioting to the outside as the player goes to the floor, or (3) the knee pivoting to the inside (as in the roll) as the player makes contact with the floor. Often the knees will come in contact with the floor, but it should be minimal and with kneepads no injury will result. The arms are stretched out and after contact with the ball, preferably with both arms, the hands are placed on the floor and allowed to slide to stretch the body full length on the floor and to absorb the landing. Sometimes the hands will still be held together and elbows will bend slightly to give the proper angle of lift.

Sprawl Review

> Stay low to the floor.
> Extend your body with a long step.
> Play the ball with both arms.
> Allow the arms to slide along the floor as the body flattens out.
> Get up quickly for next action.

TEAM SKILLS

Team Skills

The Team Skills section will deal with six people on the court and how they work together in offensive patterns, team defense, and transitional aspects of the game.

The court is commonly divided into six positions.

At the start of the game the six players assume a certain rotational order which is similar to the court positions. Note the players rotate clockwise during the game through the court positions.

Offense

Basic to any team skill is its service receive formation and the offensive formations that it uses. There are three basic offenses that are in popular use today. In each offense there are different SERVE RECEIVE FORMATIONS that are employed depending on the rotational position of each player. From these Serve Receive formations, OFFENSIVE PLAYS can be run, and HITTER COVERAGE must be employed.

One of the three basic offenses is the 4-2 system whereby two setters positioned opposite each other will handle the setting from a front

Plays, like the X, require teamwork and timing.

court position. Simplicity is the beauty of this system which relies on the power of your hitters.

A 6-2 system similarly has two setters positioned opposite each other, but the setting will be done by the setter coming from the backcourt. This system's advantage is always having three attackers in the front court.

The 5-1 system uses only one setter who does all the setting. It can be a clever mixing of both the two-hitter and three-hitter attacks while having the advantage of consistency of setting coming from a single setter.

Serve Receive Formations

Serve receive formations are important to the success of any team earning their sideout. The basic formation is a five-player receiving pattern in a W formation. Three players assume the top points of the W while the remaining two take the bottom points of the W. The setter removes herself from the pattern. The players assume different points depending on the offense and rotational positions.

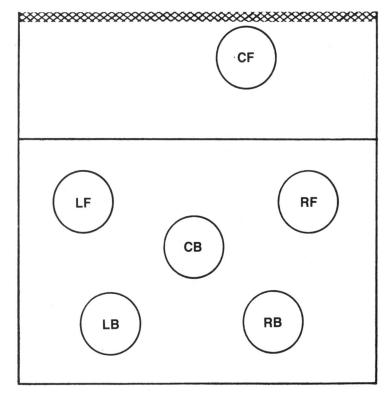

Serve Receiving Responsibilities

Areas of responsibility are designated for each player in the receiving pattern. The front spikers **must** pass most of the short serves while the deep players **must call** for the balls to inform teammates of their intentions. The various lines may move up or back to anticipate the type of serve which must be passed. At times a team may choose to receive with only four players in the passing pattern.

Rapidly becoming popular are four-player and three-player serve receive patterns. These formations are simpler because fewer players are involved, and thus fewer areas of confusion between players.

A four-player formation typically looks semicircular while a three-player formation would be more crescent shaped.

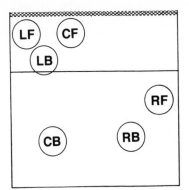 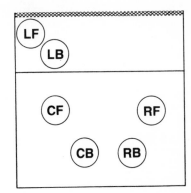

Basic 4-2 serve receive formations are shown below:

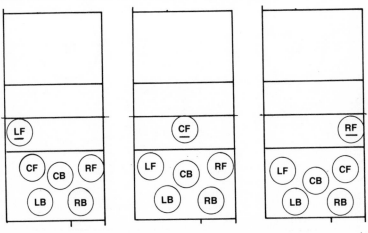

When the setter is in an outside position (LF or RF), the hitters may be moved to adjust the attack.

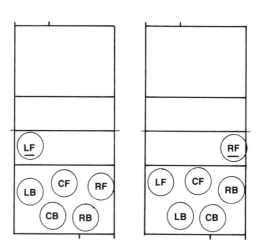

The 6-2 serve receive formations look like this:

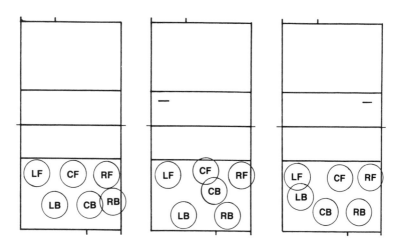

They may be varied according to your ingenuity, team ability, and the rules. Some samples are:

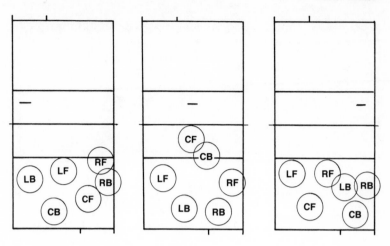

The 5-1 serve receive patterns are a combination of the 4-2 and 6-2, but usually the setter attempts to hide her positioning, especially when she is a front court player. This deception and her ability to hit the ball over on two add to the efficacy of this system.

Plays

From these formations and often in free ball situations, offenses will attempt to run plays. Good passing and teamwork are essential to run plays. Some plays include:

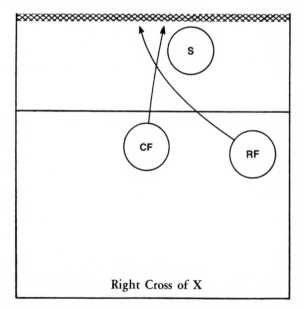

Right Cross of X

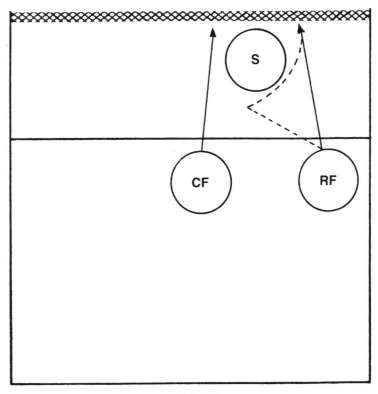

Fake X

The X and FX involve a quick set to the middle player with the right player crossing for a front 2, or faking the cross and hitting a back 2.

Some plays involving the left side player include a tandem and a left cross.

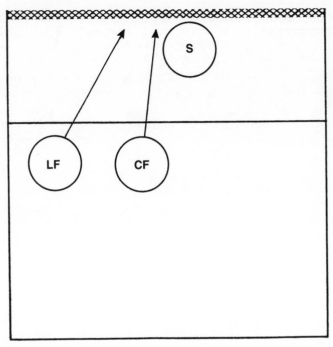

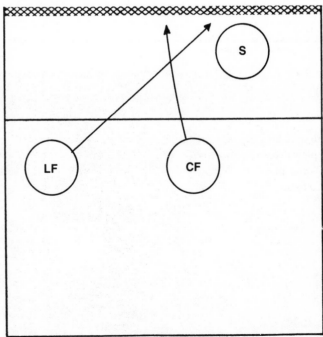

The tandem has the left front player hitting a 2 set next to the quick hitter's middle attack. In the left cross the left side player comes to hit the 1 set, while the middle hitter delays and crosses the path of the left side player to hit a 2 set.

There are many other plays that can be run, but the offense should not be made too complex for the team's skill level. Remembering that execution is the key, the plays should be designed to take advantage of your players' strengths, or your opponent's weaknesses.

Hitter Coverage

Essential to any attack is a conscientious HITTER COVERAGE system where each player covers an area of the court in case the spike is blocked. Hitter coverage is often neglected until it is too late. Players should automatically move into their respective coverage positions every time the ball is set. You must assume a low position and attempt to play the ball when it is close to the floor. This will give you more time to react to the blocked ball. You should also watch the blocker's hand so that you will see the ball coming off her hands, which will help you to react more quickly to the ball.

Most good hitter coverage systems employ two cups of coverage around the hitter. The first line of coverage has three players forming a semicircle around the hitter with the other two players filling the seams of this group.

Coverage for a 4-2 offense with the hitters outside would look like this:

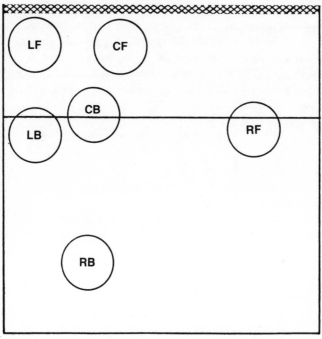

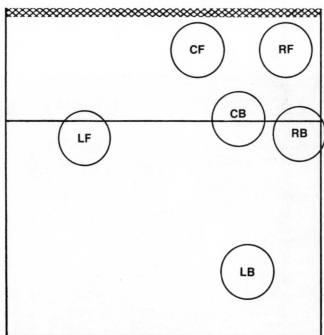

The depth of the coverage is adjustable depending on the strength of your spikers and the blockers they face. However, coverage is usually tight to the hitter since most blocked balls fall in an area around the hitter. The second row of coverage should be positioned deeper (and in the seams of the first row) to cover the remainder of the court.

In a 3 hitter attack with a backcourt setter, the coverage would look like this:

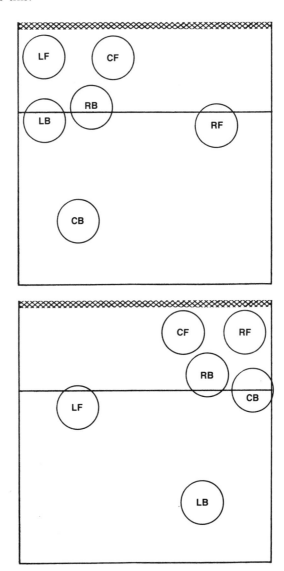

With a quick attack offense, the middle hitter should have the shortest distance to go since she will be the last player to be able to cover. However, the setter and the middle hitter's positioning could easily be switched.

Coverage of the quick middle attack is minimal since the two outside hitters are waiting for sets. The setter and backcourt players must be ready to react to a blocked ball.

Hitter coverage is a team skill and all players should know where their teammates are positioned so you won't blindly reach for a ball that your teammate can easily play. All positions of coverage must always be filled, and the hitter must also be ready to cover her own hit.

Defense

Team defense is a combination of the front court skills of blocking and the backcourt skills of digging, and the proper positioning of the players to stop your opponent's attack. Defenses are often referred to by colors and/or positioning of key players in key roles. Most common defenses are the white (man-back) and red (man-up), but increasingly popular are the blue (off-side dink coverage) defense and the rotating defense.

In all defenses there are basic starting positions, and then repositioning takes place as the ball is set to a particular hitter. When playing defense, players should constantly be adjusting their position as the ball moves so that if the ball comes into their area they will be able to move to get it.

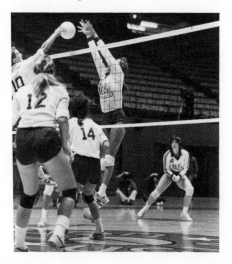

Diggers must position themselves around the block to dig effectively.

White

In the white defense, the distinguishing key player of this defense is the center back player who maintains a position deep in the court. The wing diggers, RB and LB, will normally start about halfway from the back line.

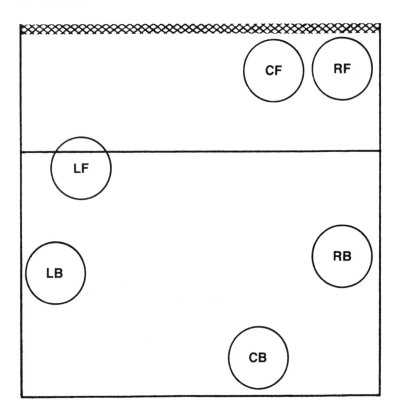

When playing against a team that runs a fast attack, these positions should be moved closer to the net to be in position to dig the quick hit.

When the ball is set, the block will form and the diggers should position themselves around the block. The RB has dink responsibility and can move up if the block has taken the line. If not she must stay and dig. The CB has responsibility for all balls deep in the court, between the blockers or off the block and must be prepared to move laterally to cover her area. The LB has the power alley just inside the block and should line up inside the shoulder of the middle blocker. The LF player should back off the net and into the court to take a sharp angle spike or balls deflected off the block in her direction.

This defense is good against strong hitting teams since there are four defenders ready to dig the ball.

Red

The red defense is distinguished by a backcourt player moving into the midcourt area to cover all dinks. This can be any player but will be described here as the CB player.

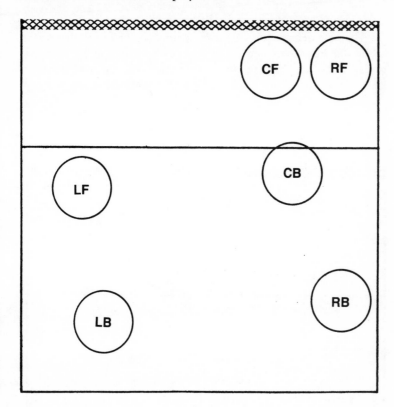

The CB will start in a position in the middle of the court about 12-15 feet off the net. As the ball is set, she moves with it to take a position in the seam of the block just behind the 10-foot line. This gives her some vision and allows her to cover a wide range. The blockers must come together properly and protect the middle areas of the court. The back court players start deep in the court (8-10' from the back line) and hold that position. The RB must be ready to dig the line and go after balls hit deep in her third of the court. The LB also starts deep and adjusts into the court slightly so that she is off the shoulder of the middle blocker. She must be ready to dig all balls hit over the block or deep crosscourt in the corner. The off-side blocker must quickly get off the net to dig the angle spike and should be at least 12-15' off the net.

This defense is excellent for good blocking teams, and is effective against teams that dink frequently. It also allows for a quick transition to offense if your "up" player is your setter.

Blue

The blue defense (off-side coverage) marks the front court player not blocking as the distinguishing player who is responsible for dink coverage. Starting positions are similar to the white defense, but once the ball is set the player not blocking slides along the net to position herself to cover behind the block.

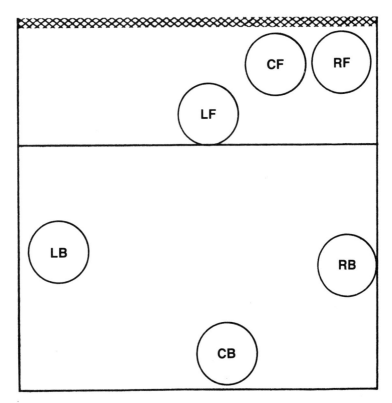

The RB player can stay deep to dig the line, knowing that the dinks will be covered by the LF player. The CB player has deep responsibility and must stay deep. The LB must dig the crosscourt angle and should line up against the middle blocker's shoulder. The LF player must move toward the opposite side of the court, staying low so as not to obstruct the LB digger. She should be about 8' off the net and at least halfway across the court. She must watch the hitter and go after the ball when it is dinked. If it is spiked she must quickly return to her hitting positon.

The defense allows for good digging coverage and gives up only that area which is hardest to hit, while having good dink coverage.

Rotating

The rotating defense is so named because the CB player will rotate to the corner on the same side the ball is set rather than maintaining a middle position. The defense requires good blockers to protect the middle of the court and quick reactions of the diggers. It puts the diggers in good position to dig and requires a lot of movement.

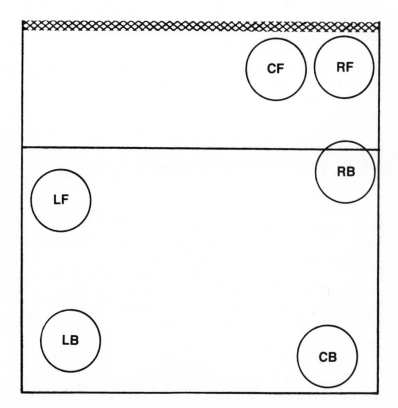

As the block forms, the RB player will move up the line to take responsibility for the dink, and the CB will move to the corner to dig the line. The LB player will rotate to the deep corner to help with the deep coverage and the LF player rotates off the net to dig the crosscourt angle. The blockers must take away the middle of the court.

Transition

Transition is that brief period of time when teams are switching from offense to defense and defense to offense. This short period is critical to the successful running of your defense or offense, and is playing an increasingly important role in determining the outcome of a game.

The transition from defense to offense involves moving quickly from hitter coverage positioning to your starting defensive position. This is usually simple enough, assuming your opponents don't make their transition quicker than you. Sometimes confusion occurs when hitters attempt to switch positions to block. This must be done quickly, or preferably not at all. It is often better to remain in your hitting positions to block, and switch only when serving, or when there is adequate time to switch.

Transition from defense to offense is more difficult since repositioning is not only necessary, but ball control must be maintained. While the dig is being made, the setter must get in position to set the ball, and the hitters must get into position (off the net) to attack. A good dig will make this easier and a simple smart set will increase the likelihood of putting the ball away.

Often a transition from your blocking position on defense to a ''down ball'' or ''free ball'' situation is called for if the opponents are unable to generate a potent attack.

A ''free ball'' situation is called for when it is apparent that the opponents will not be able to attack and must bump the ball over the net. Players should switch into their service receive formation and prepare to run the offense.

A ''down ball'' situation arises when the blockers decide that the hitter's attack will not be very potent, and the chances of digging it are good. Players quickly adjust into their down ball formation, which often is similar to a serve receive formation, and get ready to dig.

PRACTICE SKILLS AND DRILLS

Practice Skills and Drills

Practice is a very important time for a team and its players. During practice players improve their skills and the team develops its unity and personality. Rarely is a team going to be able to accomplish something in a game that they haven't already worked on in practice.

With this in mind, everyone should come into practice with set goals for accomplishing certain things. Every practice must help you improve and this is accomplished by hard work and determination.

When choosing drills for practice, coaches should pick drills that will suit their needs, and are liked by the players. This will create more enthusiasm in the practice and will lead to better results. Practice drills must incorporate repetition (the key to learning) and a success factor. This will increase the desire to continue to learn. Difficulty of the drills may be increased as the skill and success level increases.

Serve and Receive Drill

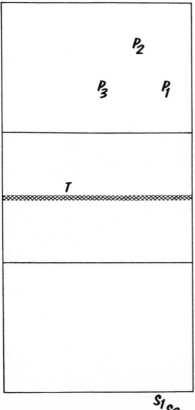

This drill incorporates serving and receiving, and you may use from 1 to 5 receivers. Players may rotate after every serve or after a specific number of good passes. Players must pass the ball to the target (T). This drill can be advanced to incorporate hitting when the pass is to the target, by having the (T) set the ball to an attacker.

Digging Drill (3 spots)

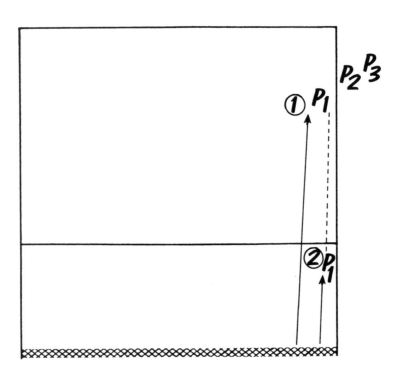

A coach, from the floor or above the net, hits a ball at player (P1) who must dig it and then move to the next position to dig another ball hit by the coach. The entire line should go across and then back, so players will practice moving in both directions. This drill can be changed slightly by making the player dig at each spot until a perfect dig is made.

Digging Drill (dig and dink)

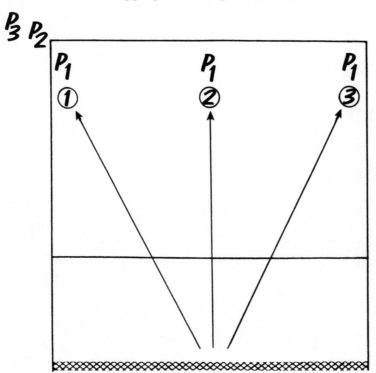

From above the net, the coach will hit a ball down the line to the player (P1) and then dink a second ball. The player must dig the first ball and using a dive or roll, play up the second ball. This action continues for each player in line.

Spiking Drill

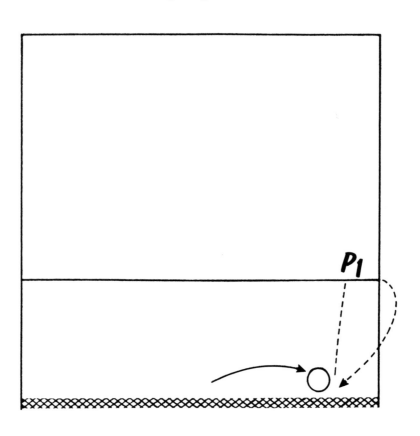

A coach will toss balls for a spiker (P1) until she hits a specific number of balls. This can be modified slightly by making the specific number exclude errors, or make the number consecutive hits in the court.

Blocking Drill

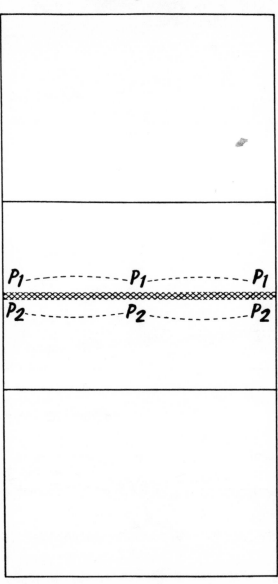

Players match up (P1 and P2) and move across the net using the slide-step or crossover step and jump and block together at the ends and the middle of the court. Players should touch hands above the net and avoid netting. It can be varied by having one player (P2) hold a ball and jump, and make the other player (P1) reach across the net to touch the ball in a blocking manner. Players can also hand the ball back and forth above the net to vary the drill slightly.

Setting Drill No. 1

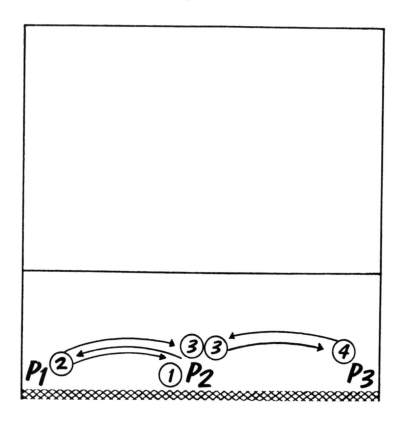

Using the overhand pass, P1 sets the ball to P2 who front sets it back to P1. P1 again sets the ball to P2 who now backsets the ball to P3. P2 turns around while P3 sets the ball to P2. This same action continues and players should periodically be rotated. This develops good front and back setting skills.

Setting Drill No. 2

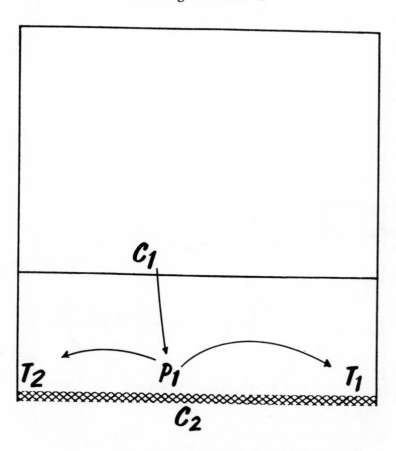

A coach (*C1*) repeatedly tosses balls to the setter (*P1*) who must front set (*T1*) or back set (*T2*) the ball upon the coach's command. The difficulty can be increased by delaying the verbal command. To teach the setters to look for the opponent's blockers, an additional person (*C2*) can be placed across the net from the setter. This person will point in the direction the ball should be set. This will teach the setter to look for blockers before setting the ball.

Dig-Hit Drill

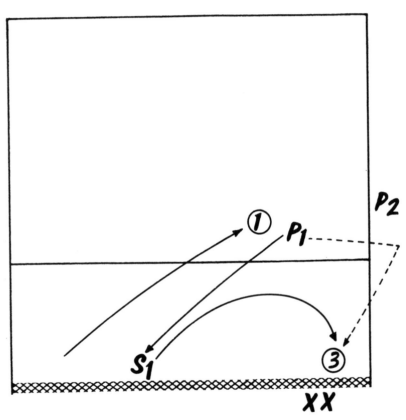

This drill combines digging and hitting and is a good transition practice drill. The coach hits a ball at the player (*P1*) who must dig it so the setter (*S1*) can set it. The setter will set *P1*, who must now spike the ball. Then *P2* follows. One or two blockers may be added to increase the difficulty of the drill. Remember to have the setter cover the hitter.

DRILLS

Drills

Three types of drills are presented in this chapter. The first set of drills is aimed at developing form. The second set should help integrate form into moving situations. The third set of drills stresses competitive play so that the player can get immediate feedback concerning her strengths and weaknesses.

Form Drills

In the form drills the player is attempting to develop a form or rhythm to carry into competitive situations. In this type of drill, time should not be a factor and the ball should be presented to the player in such a manner that she has the best chance of receiving the ball in the best possible form.

Setting/Forearm Pass Drill

OBJECT: To develop form on the set or the forearm pass.

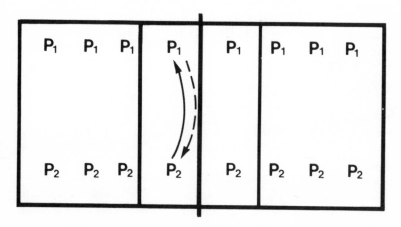

DESCRIPTION: Players are in pairs parallel to the net. P1 throws a two-hand underhand toss, giving P2 an easy, ideal opportunity to either set or pass the ball.

FEEDBACK: As players become better, the drill can be made competitive. After P1 tosses the ball she raises her hands to form a target for P2. P2 receives ten tosses and P1 scores the successes.

EQUIPMENT: One ball for each pair of players; twelve pairs of players per court.

Three-Set Drill
OBJECT: To practice three commonly used types of sets.

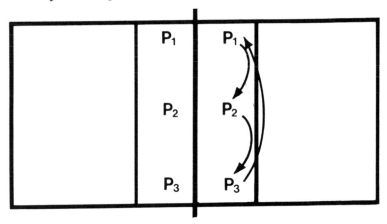

DESCRIPTION: The players group three in a line parallel to the net. *P1* sets a normal set to *P2*. *P2* backsets to *P3*. *P3* then sets across the court to *P1* and the drill continues. Players exchange positions on instructions from the coach.

FEEDBACK: Each player should be standing in a target area. If the ball is not set into the target area, the receiver of that set comments on the error.

EQUIPMENT: One ball for each group of three; six groups per court.

Diving-Rolling Drill
OBJECT: To practice diving without a ball. This is also a good warm-up drill.

DESCRIPTION: Players line up, reasonably spread out, in the defensive ready position. On a hand signal from the coach, players roll right, roll left or dive forward. Players recover immediately to ready position for the next signal from the coach.

This drill should not be used to teach diving since enthusiastic, inexperienced players often injure themselves.

FEEDBACK: Coach comments.

EQUIPMENT: Any playing surface.

Blocking Drill
OBJECT: To develop blocking form. Also a warm-up drill.

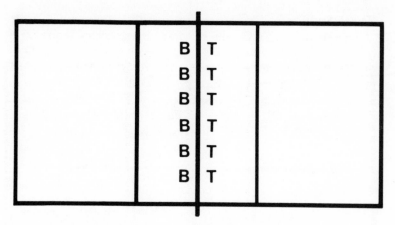

DESCRIPTION: Players pair on opposite sides of the net. Coach calls: "Ready, block." Using proper blocking techniques, blockers jump, clap hands over the top of the net and recover without fouling. As blockers improve, the coach designates one partner the blocker and the other target. Target jumps at will and "soft" blocks. Blocker jumps with the target, attack blocks over the net and claps the hands of the target.

FEEDBACK: Blockers count whether hands clap over the net. Penalty jumps are given for blocking fouls.

EQUIPMENT: One net properly secured. Six pairs of blockers can jump at one time.

Pepper Drill

OBJECT: To practice the forearm pass and spiking control.

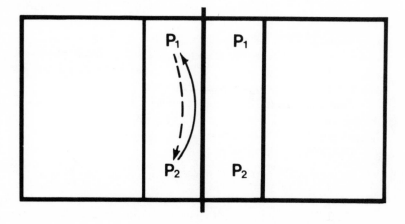

DESCRIPTION: Players are in pairs parallel to the net. P*1*, while standing in position, tosses the ball; then using spiking form, hits a nice easy top-spin hit toward P*2*. P*2* is in low ready-to-forearm-pass position. P*2* passes the ball back to P*1* who catches the ball and repeats the drill. As players develop greater passing skill, the hits may be made more difficult so that diving and rolling will be necessary.

FEEDBACK: P*1* can count the number of good passes.

EQUIPMENT: One ball per pair; twelve pairs per court.

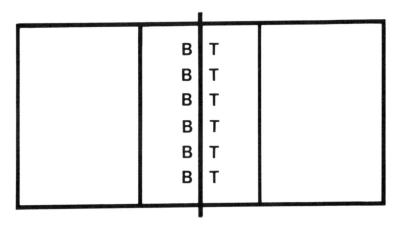

MOVEMENT DRILLS

Once the player has developed some type of form, it is necessary to integrate the form into a moving or semi-competitive situation. The player should be challenged to move and yet have ample opportunity to work and develop good form.

Sits Drill

OBJECT: To develop agility, setting control and accuracy.

DESCRIPTION: The player sets the ball to (herself) as many consecutive times as possible. On the first set, the player stands in normal setting position. On the next set, the player sits on the floor. Alternate until player misses the ball.

FEEDBACK: Player keeps track of the number of controlled sets before a miss.

EQUIPMENT: One ball.

Weave Drill

OBJECT: To develop digging skills along with endurance.

DESCRIPTION: Three players stand in a single-file line in a corner of the gym facing the coach. Other players act as shaggers or retrievers. The coach hits top-spin shots at P1 going to the right, P2 to the left, P3 to the right, P1 to the left, and so on. The drill continues for a specified time — one minute — or until the group successfully digs a given number of balls.

FEEDBACK: Counting successes gives the drill a goal. Verbal feed-

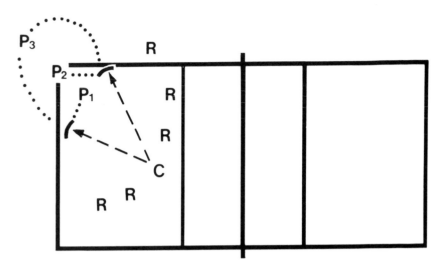

back from the coach and shaggers encourages diggers to greater effort and success.

EQUIPMENT: A minimum of six balls per drill. Six groups of three may easily be worked in a group. For large groups, one drill on each side of the net.

Two-Minute Drill

OBJECT: To practice connecting digging into offense and to develop endurance.

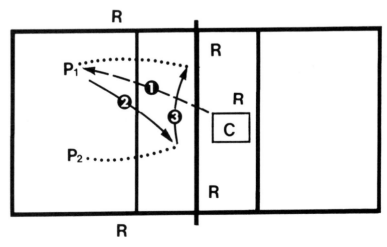

DESCRIPTION: The coach stands on a table with a shagger and ball supply nearby. *P1* and *P2* are a doubles team who must dig, set and attack the ball. Shaggers or retrievers are stationed around the court. The drill continues for a given time — two minutes — or until a given number of successful plays have been accomplished.

FEEDBACK: Either keeping score or verbal feedback from the retrievers and coach.

EQUIPMENT: One table and at least six balls. Six doubles teams can easily be worked using one court. If there are more players use triple teams.

Spatial Orientation/Setting Drill

OBJECT: To develop setting ability from any position on the court and to develop spatial orientation on the court.

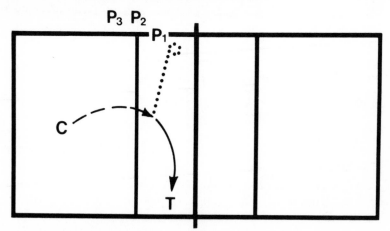

DESCRIPTION: Coach tosses ball into the air. *P1*, standing on sidelines, runs to setting position, faces target and sets ball correctly. *P2* and *P3* follow in line. *P1* replaces T, T returns ball to coach and enters line behind *P3*.

Coach tosses ball at various heights and distances from *P1* to challenge setters according to their abilities. When *P*s becomes fairly accurate with sets, the drill is varied:

1. As coach tosses ball, *P1* makes a 360° pivot, locates ball and runs to set.
2. As coach tosses ball, *P1* locates ball, makes a 180° pivot, and backsets to T.
3. T is eliminated from the drill and *P2* then serves at T. Coach tosses ball, *P1* pivots 360°, locates ball, backsets to *P2*.

.4. Do same drills with forearm pass.

FEEDBACK: T always comments on set.

EQUIPMENT: One ball; four to ten players; two drills per count.

Spatial Orientation/Spiking Drill

OBJECT: To teach the spiker to correctly respond to various types of sets.

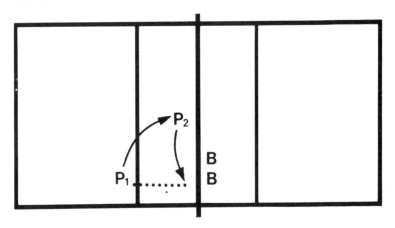

DESCRIPTION: One spiker attacks five to ten consecutive sets. Spiker P*1* tosses ball to P*2* who is in setter's position. Setter gives various types of sets to spiker who is expected to play the ball correctly. On good sets, the kill is expected; on deep sets, the attack must be kept in play; on unhittable sets, the ball must be saved; and on sets over the net, the ball must be blocked. The drill is not designed for endurance, but it can be made an endurance drill if the balls are tossed rapidly. Retrievers return ball to tosser. A blocker and/or a digger may be added to this drill.

FEEDBACK: The number of correct plays are recorded. The coach gives verbal feedback.

EQUIPMENT: Six balls; four to eight players per drill; two drills per court.

COMPETITIVE DRILLS

Competitive drills should be as game-like as possible so players will get immediate feedback on the success or failure of their performance.

Three-Point Game Drill

OBJECT: To practice serving and receiving and to create pressure in serving and receiving.

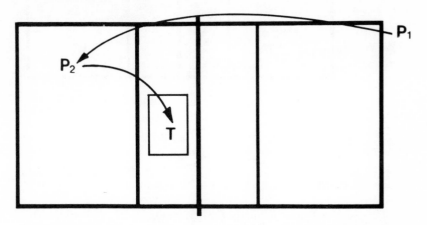

DESCRIPTION: P*1* must serve into one half-court. P*2* must defend that half-court. T is the target and scorekeeper. The coach chooses an ideal target area into which the ball must be passed. Good passes must be in the target area and must be settable. P*1* and P*2* compete against each other.

When a player wins the game, she no longer ''needs'' practice in that skill and switches positions with T. The loser ''needs'' practice and stays in that position until she wins or until the coach suggests mercy.

FEEDBACK: To win a game, a player must win three consecutive points. The passer scores only when the pass made is settable in the target area or when the server makes a service error. (The serve must be in the half-court designated.) The server wins a point if the passer fails to pass into the ideal target area.

EQUIPMENT: One ball per drill; three players per drill; two drills per court.

Instant Loser Drill

OBJECT: To have a coach-controlled competitive game with lots of activity for the players.

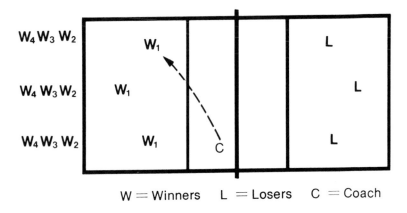

W = Winners   L = Losers   C = Coach

DESCRIPTION: The coach stands at the sidelines near the net with a large supply of balls. Players are grouped in teams of two or three. The "losing team is on the opposite side of the net behind the coach. The "winning" teams groups at the back of the court on the coach's side of the net.

Coach spikes the winning team. Winners dig, set and attack. The point is played out between the two teams on the court. The losing team immediately gets ready for defense against the next winning team. Winners return the ball to the coach.

SCORING: There are many variations of scoring.
1. If winners fail to get the coach's spike to the defending team, winners get "minus one" and fall in at the end of the winner's line. Minus two against the same opponent is a loss and the team goes to the loser's side.
2. If winners get coach's spike to the loser's side of the court, the point is played. The loser of this is an "instant loser" and goes to, or remains on, the losing side.

EQUIPMENT: Six balls; nine to 18 players; one game per court.

Concentration Drill

OBJECT: To create pressure situations, to develop consistency and concentration and to force teams to discover and work on their weaknesses.

DESCRIPTION: Two teams are chosen, usually first team against second team. One team will **always** serve. Normal points are played.

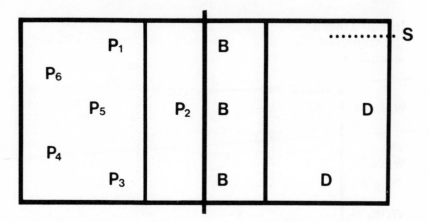

SCORING: The coach decides on scoring goals and which team needs extra pressure. Coach also decides which team needs work on passing and offense while the other works on serving and defense. For example:

> (1) The receiving team rotates only if it scores three consecutive "side-outs" and (2) The serving team rotates only if it scores two consecutive "points."

The team who rotates six positions first wins the competition.

EQUIPMENT: Normal game equipment.

Rule of Eighteen Drill

OBJECT: To create pressure sooner in a game situation, to quickly terminate lopsided games, and to encourage outstanding play by rewarding good play with quick victory.

DESCRIPTION: Normal game play.

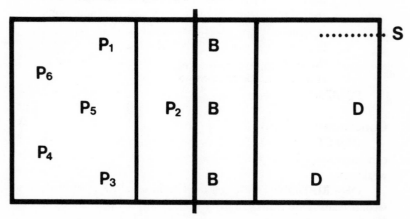

SCORING: A game terminates when the winner's score plus the difference in score between the teams equals 18 (or 19). Thus victorious scores are:

9-0	
10-1, 10-2	14-9, 14-10
11-3, 11-4	15-11, 15-12
12-5, 12-6	16-13, 16-14
13-7, 13-8	17-15, 17-16

EQUIPMENT: Normal game equipment.

Ping Pong Scoring Drill

OBJECT: To allow players to work on all phases of the game without getting "stuck" in one position.

DESCRIPTION: Normal game play.

SCORING: Each player serves five times. A point is scored on every serve (either for the serving team or for the receiving team). Thirty-one

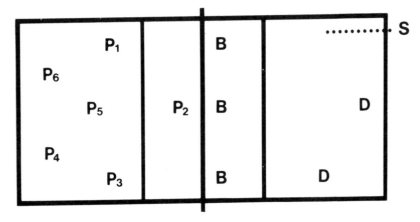

points is game. If deuce, each player serves only one ball until one team has a two-point lead.

EQUIPMENT: Normal game equipment.

A WORD ON TRAINING AND NUTRITION

A Word on Training and Nutrition

In this final section I would like to mention two other topics that are important to every volleyball player. Nutrition and training play an important role in the life of every athlete, and further inquiries on these topics should be made to give you a good understanding of their value to you.

Training

As in any sport, volleyball players must train if they hope to reach their potential and be distinguished from a recreational athlete. In addition to practicing the skills particular to our sport, they must also work to develop strength and conditioning. All volleyball players should develop a strength and conditioning program that is suitable for them.

Strength is necessary because of the demands our sport puts on our body. Leg strength is necessary for the repetitive jumping that is involved in spiking and blocking, and for the ability to maintain a low defensive position. Upper body strength is necessary for the arm actions of spiking and blocking, and to absorb the body's weight when diving to the floor. Strength and flexibility of your muscles will also help to limit your injuries and their seriousness.

Conditioning is also very important to help you maintain your quickness and strength throughout each game, each match, and each tournament. Aerobic and anerobic training should be undertaken to get into the best possible condition.

Nutrition

Nutrition is another important aspect all volleyball players should heed. Because of the demands that you put on your body, you should be sure to refuel it with proper foods and maintain a well-balanced diet. A volleyball player does not need to be over-nourished or underfed. Every athlete should find out the right kinds of food needed to maintain a balanced diet that will provide enough energy for the body.

GLOSSARY

Glossary of Power Volleyball Terms

ATTACK: The act of jumping into the air to hit the ball from above the level of the net into the opponents court.

BLOCK: A defensive play by one or more players who attempt to intercept the ball as it passes over the net. In power volleyball it is legal for the blockers to reach over the net to block the ball as soon as the attack is made.

DEFENSE: The action by a team when the ball is controlled by its opponents. Defense is primarily a matter of team tactics. However, there are certain individual techniques which attempt to convert the defense to the offense. These include the **block,** the **dig,** the **dive** and the **roll.** (Some authorities consider the **serve reception** in this category.)

DIG: Recovery of an opponent's attack made by playing the ball with one or both hands or arms.

DINK: An attack in which the ball is hit with little force from the fingertips or fist. There are many interpretations as to the legality of the various techniques for the dink.

DIVE: A defensive technique employed to increase the forward range of motion. The defensive player dives forward, recovers a difficult shot, then lands upon her chest and abdomen after being cushioned by hands and arms.

FOREARM PASS: A ball played in an underhand manner. The forearms, held away from the body, act as a surface from which the pass can be made.

FOUL: An encroachment of the rules or a failure to play the ball properly as permitted under the rules.

GAME: To win a game, a team must score 15 points and be ahead by at least two points. If the score reaches 14-14, play continues until the winner achieves a two-point advantage. However, it is sometimes necessary to use time limits or other maximum scores to determine the winner.

OFFENSE: The action by the team controlling the ball. Offensive techniques include the **serve,** the **serve reception,** the **set** and the **attack.**

OVERHAND OR FACE PASS: A ball played from in front of the face with the fingertips of both hands. The hands must be in such a position that the passer is able to see the back of her hands.

OVERLAP: A foul committed as players stand in incorrect rotational order before the ball is served. No player may infringe on the territory of a player immediately adjacent to her. For instance, **player F** has only three players immediately adjacent to her. She must remain behind **player C** and in between **player E** and **A.** In the patterns of power volleyball, the interpretations of overlap become relatively complex.

PASS: The controlled movement of the ball usually from one player to another on the same team. It may be either a forearm pass or an overhand pass. Usually this term is applied to the first play of the ball after it has crossed the net and often is applied only to the serve reception.

PLAY-OVER: A play-over is the act of putting the ball into play again without awarding a point or a side-out.

POINT: A point is awarded to the serving team only when the receiving team commits a foul.

POWER VOLLEYBALL: A game distinguished from recreational volleyball by the amount of organization needed for highly refined implementation of team strategy and individual skills. It is a game for players who possess a certain amount of quickness, alertness, coordination and stamina, and who desire to further develop the same.

ROLL: A defensive technique employed to increase the sideward range of motion. The defensive player lunges sideward, recovers a difficult shot then rolls over the back and shoulder to regain a defensive position.

SERVE: The technique in which the ball is put into play. Serves may be classified in many ways. If classified by arm swing, they are the **underhand, overhand** and **roundhouse serves.** If classified by ball movement, they are **spin serves** and **floating serves.** Most power volleyball players use some form of the floating serve.

SET: A pass, made overhand or underhand, hit into the air for the purpose of placing the ball in position for the attack. Normally the set is the second hit by the offensive team.

SIDE-OUT: Side-out shall be declared and the ball given to the opponents to serve when the serving team commits a foul. Points are not scored on a side-out.

SOFT SPIKE: An attack in which the ball is hit at less than maximum force to gain some tactical advantage.

SPIKE: An attack in which the ball is hit with great force.

Drill Keys

P = Player Performing Drill
C = Coach

Path of Player's Movement

B = Blockers
S = Server
T = Target